Elusive Equity:

A Report on Superintendents' Perceptions of the Participation of Eligible Catholic School Students and Teachers in *Elementary and Secondary Education Act* Programs

ACE Consulting
UNIVERSITY OF NOTRE DAME

Edited by
Stephen Perla
Michelle Doyle
Charles Lamphier

Alliance for Catholic Education Press
at the University of Notre Dame

Notre Dame, Indiana

Alliance for Catholic Education Press
at the University of Notre Dame
158 IEI Building
Notre Dame, IN 46556
http://www.nd.edu/~acepress

Text design by Julie Wernick Dallavis
Cover design by Mary Jo Adams Kocovski

ISBN 978-0-9819501-5-0

TABLE OF CONTENTS

ACKNOWLEDGMENTS

ACE Consulting wishes to warmly thank Mary Ann Remick who continues to make a lasting positive impact on Catholic education through her support of this report.

ACE Consulting also wishes to thank the National Catholic Educational Association Department of Chief Administrators of Catholic Education for assistance in the research that made this report possible.

Executive Summary

Answering a call from the United States Bishops for institutions of higher education to commit themselves more deeply to the success of Catholic K-12 schools, Notre Dame President Fr. John Jenkins, C.S.C., commissioned the Notre Dame Task Force on Catholic Education in 2005. Chaired by Fr. Timothy Scully, C.S.C., the Task Force brought together over fifty leaders of diverse backgrounds and expertise in a year-long effort to study the challenges and opportunities facing Catholic schools and to develop a strategic plan for improving the viability and effectiveness of these schools. The Task Force's Final Report, *Making God Known, Loved, and Served: The Future of Catholic Primary and Secondary Schools in the United States*, articulates twelve recommendations for Notre Dame to extend and enhance its commitment to Catholic schools.

The Task Force recommended that, consistent with its character as a Catholic institution of higher learning and research, Notre Dame commit to the careful analysis of the degree to which Catholic school students and teachers are able to claim the benefits of the federal grant programs to which they are entitled, and through education and expert guidance, to support Catholic school leaders as they seek to access the benefits of these programs on behalf of students and teachers.

To this end, ACE Consulting, under the auspices of the University of Notre Dame's Alliance for Catholic Education (ACE), formed a partnership with the National Catholic Educational Association (NCEA) and its Department of Chief Administrators of Catholic Education (CACE). CACE encourages its regional groupings of Catholic school superintendents to organize annual or semi-annual regional meetings. Through cooperation between NCEA, CACE, and ACE Consulting, staff from

ACE gathered input on the experiences of diocesan staff and their school principals seeking equitable participation in federal grant programs, especially the Elementary and Secondary Education Act (ESEA), currently named the No Child Left Behind Act (NCLB).

ACE visited with each region. During these regional meetings with Catholic school superintendents, ACE gathered input on the experiences of diocesan staff and their school principals seeking equitable participation in federal grant programs, especially the *Elementary and Secondary Education Act* (ESEA), currently named the *No Child Left Behind Act* (NCLB). ACE Consulting gathered qualitative and anecdotal data from approximately 150

Catholic school administrators from nearly every diocese in the nation on a wide range of issues related to ESEA.

These listening sessions were staffed principally by two individuals from ACE Consulting. Steve Perla, the Director of ACE Consulting, came to Notre Dame from the Diocese of Worcester, Massachusetts, where he served as Superintendent of Catholic Schools. Previously, Perla spent eleven years as the Executive Director of the Parents Alliance for Catholic Education (PACE), the Massachusetts advocacy organization for Catholic schools. While at PACE, Catholic schools in Massachusetts saw a 200 percent increase in federal education benefits to their students. Michelle Doyle, who served as a consultant on this project, is the former education lobbyist for the United States Conference of Catholic Bishops (USCCB). Previously, Doyle was the Director of the Office on Non-Public Education at the United States Department of Education. She also has experience as a Catholic school teacher, principal, and central office administrator.

The findings from the Listening Sessions validated what Catholic school leaders suspected: Despite the clear intent of Congress for private school students and teachers to participate equitably in many ESEA programs, equitable participation has not been experienced by most Catholic schools. Instead, the reports from the field overwhelmingly

The findings from the Listening Sessions validated what Catholic school leaders suspected: Despite the clear intent of Congress for private school students and teachers to participate equitably in many ESEA programs, equitable participation has not been experienced by most Catholic schools.

demonstrate that Congress' legislative prerogatives are not being met. Despite the law's intent for these programs to be student-centered, collaborative, and transparent, nearly every Catholic school superintendent who participated in the listening sessions reported that this is not the case in practice. This report details this unfortunate situation and describes the role that ACE Consulting intends to play in addressing the challenges faced by the Catholic school community.

Introduction to Private School Participation in the *Elementary and Secondary Education Act*

Since 1965, when Congress first passed the *Elementary and Secondary Education Act*, students enrolled in private schools have been eligible to participate in certain federal education programs. Likewise, federal law has long permitted private school teachers to participate in many of the same government programs as their public school counterparts. The current authorization of ESEA, known as the *No Child Left Behind Act*, maintains the long-standing policy that children and teachers in private schools must be provided with equitable participation in most programs authorized under ESEA.

As the law is constructed, public school districts bear the responsibility for serving eligible children, regardless of where they attend school, and retain fiscal control of all federal funds. Private schools never receive federal dollars under ESEA; rather, students and teachers benefit by participating in programs which are funded by federal statute. To ensure that the program of services meets the needs of eligible children attending private schools, the public school district must initiate and conduct a process of consultation.

With nearly 2.2 million students currently enrolled, Catholic schools represent the largest private school system in the nation. Serving schools marked by religious, economic, and racial diversity, Catholic schools attend to a tremendous national need. With 42 percent of Catholic schools located in either urban or inner-city environments, the system has embraced the mission of serving the poor, the immigrant, and the marginalized, regardless of social status or religious affiliation. In fact, more than 51 percent of schools serve children who qualify for services under ESEA's Title I program, which aims at improving the academic achievement of

The current authorization of ESEA, known as the No Child Left Behind Act, maintains the long-standing policy that children and teachers in private schools must be provided with equitable participation in most programs authorized under ESEA.

disadvantaged students, and 50 percent of schools participate in Federal Nutrition Programs. At the same time, Catholic schools have shown remarkable results: The National Catholic Educational Association reports that 99 percent of Catholic school secondary students graduate and 81 percent go on to a four-year college. All these feats are accomplished while saving the taxpayers billions of dollars that would be required by increased enrollments in public schools.[1]

The Intent of Congress Regarding the Participation of Private School Students and Teachers in ESEA Programs

The decision of parents to enroll their children in private schools does not disqualify those children from participating in most federal programs administered by public school districts. Congress grants funds for these programs to the states, which in turn subgrants funds to public school districts, referred to in the law as local educational agencies (LEAs). These school districts, then, are charged with the administration of the ESEA programs to benefit children who are enrolled in public schools and, through a consultation process, those who are enrolled in private schools. Congress, through legislation, and the United States Department of Education, through regulations and guidance in the administration of the law, have laid out clear procedures for ensuring the equitable participation of private school students in federal education programs. The legislation and guidance clearly call for equitable services to private school students to be student-centered, collaborative, and transparent.

STUDENT–CENTERED

All federal education programs have one central aim: ensure that each student is able to achieve high standards of learning and academic excellence. In providing services to private school students and teachers, the needs of private school students provide the foundation for program design. In many cases, the needs of public and private school students vary widely. Therefore, LEAs may not simply invite private schools to participate in programs aimed at servicing the public school community. Rather, school districts are required to consult with private school officials so that the needs of their students are met through the program services.[2]

The decision of parents to enroll their children in private schools does not disqualify those children from participating in most federal programs administered by public school districts.

In an effort to better serve the needs of private school students, the law allows LEAs to contract with third-party providers for the delivery of services. These school districts are to be applauded for their commitment to student-centeredness when such an arrangement can result in the educational needs of private school students being met in a manner that is more efficient and effective, creating a student-centered program to deliver equitable services.[3]

COLLABORATIVE

The U.S. Supreme Court has upheld the constitutionality of federal education program benefits for private school students by relying on the requirement that control of the program be maintained by the public entity.[4] Because of this important reality, Congress has mandated that school districts engage in "timely and meaningful consultation" with private school officials to determine the best way to deliver services to their students and educators.[5]

The consultation process is designed to provide a collaborative setting in which children's needs are discussed and the uses of resources allocated through federal grant programs for private school children are considered and agreed upon. Ideally, these consultation meetings take place with ample planning and at mutually acceptable times for both public and private school officials. Clearly, if the intention of these meetings is to collaborate, it is ideal for both the public and private school officials to be able to participate in discussions after having an opportunity to gather all appropriate data and be in a position to make important decisions.[6]

In many areas, Catholic school leaders have found it expedient and in the best interest of the children in their care if consultation takes place between the public school district and one individual from the central Catholic schools office on behalf of all the schools in the district. The law clearly allows for this kind of arrangement, as it leads to efficiency and allows principals to focus more directly on the daily educational needs of their students and schools.[7]

TRANSPARENT

Local school districts are expected to allocate resources to the private school program in a manner that is open and honest. Additionally, it is clear that the new Administration and Congress are placing a high value on transparency regarding the allocation and utilization of federal funding. To this end,

school districts should determine the per pupil allocation—the funding generated by public and private school students—fairly and transparently, taking into account the appropriate data developed through consultation with private school officials.[8]

Congress has mandated that school districts engage in "timely and meaningful consultation" with private school officials to determine the best way to deliver services to their students and educators.

School districts apply to the state for subgrants from ESEA programs by completing a consolidated application or individual applications for each program. Transparency is best achieved when these applications require the district to clearly delineate the allocation of federal dollars for public and private school children. The applications are public documents and are required to be provided to any private school official upon request. They are created by each state in accordance with the requirements of ESEA, although currently there is no specific obligation to break out the funding between the public and private school programs in the LEAs' applications to the state.[9]

Since public school officials must maintain program and fiscal control, they are also responsible for the administration of ESEA. The law does not require that private school officials provide any administrative support to the public school district in order to have their students participate in programs. On the contrary, the law charges the school district with the administration of ESEA, and requires public school officials to serve eligible private school children through an open collaboration with private school personnel.[10]

Report from Listening Sessions

In order to judge the effectiveness of the *No Child Left Behind Act* in serving children attending Catholic schools, ACE Consulting conducted ten listening sessions which sought the input from superintendents of Catholic schools across the nation on a wide variety of issues related to the administration of federal grant programs and their ability to gain participation for their students and teachers. Most superintendents expressed extreme frustration and reported that the obstacles placed in the path to their students' and teachers' participation in federal grant programs seemed insurmountable. In fact, some Catholic school leaders believe public school districts intentionally stymie their efforts to gain participation in federal grant programs, thereby allowing school districts to retain the funds allocated for private school students and teachers. Put succinctly, the vast majority of superintendents reported that the equitable services required by *No Child Left Behind* were not being provided.

STUDENT–CENTERED

Catholic school leaders frequently reported that the needs of Catholic school students were not considered during program design. Rather, in too many cases, public school districts simply allow Catholic school students to participate in their predetermined programs without considering the unique needs of Catholic school students. In fact, superintendents reported that their students and teachers were treated as afterthoughts, instead of as equal participants in federal programs. Many times Catholic school students were invited to participate in programs "if there is room."

Most superintendents expressed extreme frustration and reported that the obstacles placed in the path to their students' and teachers' participation in federal grant programs seemed insurmountable.

Another concern is that private school students have generated funds for which they have no access to services. The Title I program as currently written into law requires that districts reserve certain percentages of funds for specific uses. Only after these set asides have been calculated does the district determine the proportional funding for private school students. In some instances when a district is in improvement status under NCLB, 40 percent of the Title I allocation is taken off the top for required reservations with little or no benefit for the private school program.

Superintendents reported that appropriate options are not available for an equitable opportunity for students to receive equitable services. As a proposed remedy to the lack of attention to student-centeredness, many Catholic school leaders reported that they asked their school district to contract

Catholic school leaders frequently reported that the needs of Catholic school students were not considered during program design.

with a third-party provider for services. While the law allows for the use of third parties, and many Catholic school officials find that third parties provide better services more targeted to the needs of participating Catholic school students, many districts refuse even to consider the use of a third party. It should be noted that the law requires districts to give thorough consideration to the views of private school officials on the use of third-party providers.

COLLABORATIVE

NCLB requires that public and private school officials consult in order to determine the most appropriate programs for addressing the needs of Catholic school students and teachers. This consultation is required to be "timely and meaningful." The listening sessions yielded numerous criticisms of the practice of consultation.

Too frequently, superintendents reported that consultation meetings were scheduled abruptly and without adequate advanced notice, offering very little time to prepare or, in some cases, even to be present at the meetings. As a result, Catholic school leaders reported that they often felt unprepared

and rushed at their consultation meetings. Without enough time to gather the appropriate data, many superintendents contend that they feel pressured into accepting the district's offer of services without being able to advocate for the specific needs of their students. Additionally, many meetings only provided information to private school officials without an opportunity for them to discuss the needs of their students and how federal program benefits could help to meet those needs. For these reasons, many Catholic school leaders argued that consultation has proven to be neither timely nor meaningful.

Because of heightened difficulties experienced by Catholic school leaders, many schools elect to allow central office administrators (such as the superintendent or an assistant superintendent charged with government-relations responsibilities) to consult with local school districts. Some school districts have refused to consult with diocesan staff and, instead, insist on working only with the building-level principal. Many Catholic school offices believe the districts do this so they can provide less service by working with Catholic school principals who tend to be less knowledgeable about the specifics of the law than professionals who deal with ESEA on a daily basis.

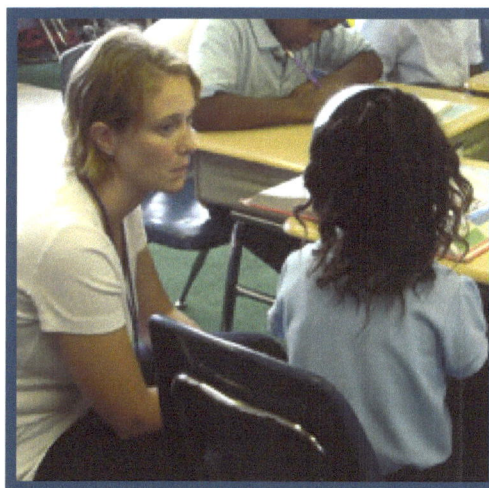

Even when the principals do attempt participation, they admit to a lack of understanding of the law and simply must believe what the public school district tells them, without having the knowledge to challenge the district's interpretation or presentation of program benefits. Superintendents and their staffs recommended that a lexicon for the layman be developed providing common definition of terms and correcting common myths about federal program services to private school students and teachers.

Compounding difficulties in collaboration, many superintendents reported that district personnel in charge of the private school program were continually changing and therefore new and inexperienced in their jobs. By the time a working relationship could be established, personnel changed again. Catholic school leaders report that their public school district counterparts often do not know the provision of the law that provides for the equitable participation of Catholic school students. New personnel deny services provided in the past with no explanation. Additionally, because dioceses work with multiple school districts for the Title I program, they report that the interpretation of what is allowed and what occurs during consultation can differ dramatically from one public school district to another.

A consistent concern expressed by diocesan officials was that the paperwork requirements for participating in these programs were extensive and often led to a school not being able have its students participate in the program. The law does not impose any paperwork requirements on private school officials, so all paperwork requests are originating with the public school districts. While some paperwork is inevitable and appropriate, superintendents reported that the amount of paperwork and limited time line for completion discouraged participation in program benefits.[11]

Lastly, dioceses incur many costs when working with public school districts to consult on federal programs. In many cases, personnel are hired by the diocese to either exclusively work on federal program participation or have program participation as a major part of their portfolio of responsibilities. The cost of these staff members currently cannot be reimbursed by federal program funds. Some cooperative districts rely on these diocesan employees to be compliant with federal requirements and to ensure the programs operate effectively. In districts that are not cooperative with private school principals in providing required services, dioceses have had to increase their personnel to ensure students' rights guaranteed by the law. Superintendents believed that reimbursement for these costs is appropriate.

Many Catholic school leaders argued that consultation has proven to be neither timely nor meaningful.

TRANSPARENT

Many superintendents report that districts do not disclose their method of determining the equitable share for private school students, or the amount of funding available for particular programs. Often the consolidated application or individual program applications, which are public documents that should spell out how resources are requested and earmarked, are not made available to private school officials, despite repeated requests. In some cases, information on the private school program is not spelled out in the applications.

Many Catholic school superintendents were unable to determine whether or not their students and teachers were receiving their fair share of services.

Superintendents expressed particular concern over transparency in the administration of Title I, designed to assist educationally needy children in areas of poverty, and Title IIA, designed for the professional development of teachers. Under Title I, Catholic school officials report that the district often assigns a resource teacher to a Catholic school for a predetermined number of hours per week, but Catholic school leaders are unable to determine if this service is in fact equitable and proportional to the number of qualifying students enrolled in their school. Additionally, because NCLB requires that students who qualify for Title I services must receive those services from the school district in which they reside, as opposed to the school district in which they attend school, many superintendents lamented the difficulty in receiving adequate information from the large number of LEAs from which many Catholic schools and dioceses draw students and noted that it was unlikely that students resid-

ing in one district and attending school in another would ever receive Title I services.

Under Title IIA, many superintendents voiced a similar concern about transparency because of a lack of clarity in whether public schools were expending funds on professional development, for which private school students generate funding for the participation of private school teachers, versus class-size reduction and teacher recruitment and retention costs, which do not apply to the private school program. Many Catholic school superintendents were unable to determine whether or not their students and teachers were receiving their fair share of services.

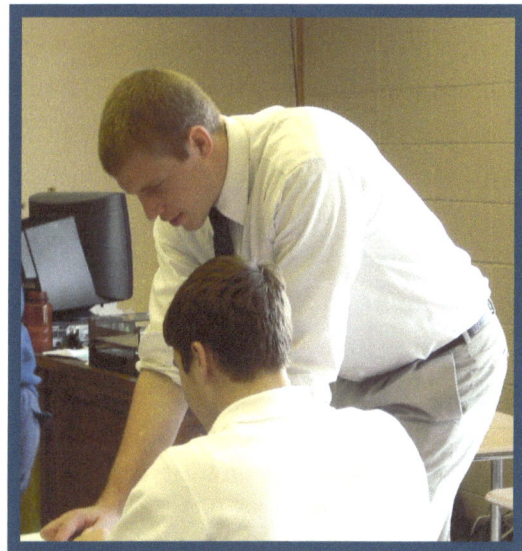

Similarly, public school districts can sometimes carry over funding from one year to another, depending on particular rules in their state and by federal program. These carryover funds should be shared equitably with the private school program the following year if they are expended for uses that require equitable participation, but superintendents report that districts usually are not willing to disclose whether or not there is carryover from one year to the next or how the funds will be used.[12]

ACE Consulting's Commitment

The results of the listening sessions gave voice to the frustrations of Catholic school leaders in the field trying to obtain equitable services for their students and teachers. Despite the clear intention of Congress, and the efforts of many devoted individuals from both the public and Catholic school communities, it is clear that many private school students are not receiving their equitable share of services under *No Child Left Behind.* ACE Consulting is committed to undertaking a multi-pronged strategy to ensure that students are treated justly.

In response to the information collected in the listening sessions, including suggestions from the superintendents about what could be done under current law to help resolve these issues, ACE Consulting presented findings to the United States Department of Education. As a result, the Department has revised its guidance document, *Equitable Services for Eligible Private School Students, Teachers, and Other Educational Personnel.* This revised guidance

ACE Consulting is committed to undertaking a multi-pronged strategy to ensure that students are treated justly.

addresses many issues raised by superintendents during the listening sessions and includes tools, sample checklists, and other useful documents that are for the use of both public and private school officials.

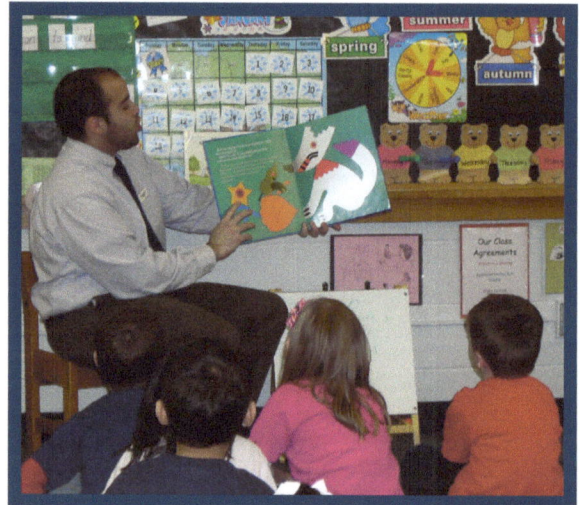

Along with the United States Conference of Catholic Bishops (USCCB), ACE Consulting has co-convened an ad hoc committee on the reauthorization of ESEA. This 21-person committee, comprised of Catholic school leaders from across the country, is providing research and suggestions to the USCCB in its efforts to favorably influence the reauthorization. In its leadership capacity of this committee, ACE is playing the traditional role of a university: providing research and offering a forum for thoughtful debate. The substance of the work of the ad hoc committee is based on the recommendations by superintendents in the listening sessions for changes to ESEA to solve the issues raised during the discussions.

ACE Consulting is also deeply committed to supporting local efforts by Catholic schools and dioceses to access their students' equitable share of federal education programs. Committed to data-driven decision making, ACE Consulting has designed a survey instrument which provides for a thorough examination of the Catholic school community's level of equitable federal grant participation. Subsequent to the diocese-wide study, ACE Consulting can provide expert guidance and assistance to help Catholic schools and dioceses successfully obtain equitable services.

Once ESEA is reauthorized, ACE Consulting plans on designing a host of resources aimed at building capacity within the Catholic school community. These resources will be a response to the call from superintendents heard in the listening sessions for training and expert guidance. Particularly, ACE Consulting intends to design written and online materials, including interactive webinars, in order to train Catholic school staff. Additionally, ACE Consulting will be available to provide in-person training and consultation.

Committed to data-driven decision making, ACE Consulting has designed a survey instrument which provides for a thorough examination of the Catholic school community's level of equitable federal grant participation. Subsequent to the diocese-wide study, ACE Consulting can provide expert guidance and assistance to help Catholic schools and dioceses successfully obtain equitable services.

Guidance from the Department of Education

The United States Department of Education has issued a number of authoritative documents which offer guidance to both the public and private school communities for their efforts to ensure equitable participation in federal grant programs for students and teachers in private schools. The footnotes in this document have made repeated references to the most recent such document. *Equitable Services for Eligible Private School Students, Teachers, and Other Educational Personnel: Non-Regulatory Guidance* was published by the Department of Education's Office of Non-Public Education in March 2009. It includes a series of questions and answers, and a host of other resources, which will assist administrators in their efforts to ensure the equitable participation of private school students and teachers in certain federal education programs. The March 2009 document applies to the administration of the following programs authorized under ESEA:

- Title I, Part B, Subpart 1, *Reading First*;
- Title I, Part B, Subpart 3, *Even Start Family Literacy*;
- Title I, Part C, *Education of Migratory Children*;
- Title II, Part A, *Teacher and Principal Training and Recruiting Fund*;

- Title II, Part B, *Mathematics and Science Partnerships*;
- Title II, Part D, *Enhancing Education through Technology*;
- Title III, Part A, *English Language Acquisition, Language Enhancement, and Academic Achievement*;
- Title IV, Part A, *Safe and Drug-Free Schools and Communities*; and
- Title IV, Part B, *21st Century Community Learning Centers*.

It does not, however, refer to the largest program currently funded by ESEA, Title I, Part A. See the table to the right for a list of useful documents and websites which will assist private school officials in understanding equitable participation for major ESEA programs.

The following are excerpts from Department of Education guidance documents which are particularly germane to the findings from ACE Consulting's listening sessions. Unless otherwise noted, the excerpts and referenced sample documents are taken from *Equitable Services for Eligible Private School Students, Teachers, and Other Educational Personnel* and can be found at the web address listed on the following page.

D-4. May a group of private school officials designate a single private school official to represent their interests?

Yes. For example, in some areas, one private school official may represent a group of private school officials in an LEA. In such a situation, the appointed private school official should inform the LEA of his or her intent to represent the group of school officials in the LEA and request that the LEA communicate directly with the appointed official.

D-5. When does consultation between public and private school officials occur?

Section 9501(c)(3) of ESEA requires that consultation between the LEA and private school officials occur before the LEA makes any decision (such as ordering materials or hiring staff) that affects the opportunities of private school children, teachers, and other educational personnel to participate in programs requiring their equitable participation. In order to ensure timely consultation, LEAs should begin the consultation process early enough in the decision-making process to allow for participation of private school students and teachers at the start of each school year. Therefore, the LEA should engage in a process of timely and meaningful consultation with private school officials and provide them with information related to the projected and/or final funding amounts for programs and services, including on the process the LEA will use in preparing its competitive grant application. The LEA should also develop a process for determining mutual expectations for implementation and assessment of programs. In order to meet the requirements for timely and meaningful consultation, many LEAs begin consultation for the following school year in mid- to late-winter of the school year prior to the year covered by the plan. For samples of timelines, see *J-3: Sample General Consultation Timeline*; and *J-4: Sample Consultation Timeline*.

D-6. How does an LEA begin the consultation process?

An LEA generally begins the consultation process each year by contacting private school officials representing the private schools located within its boundaries. One way to accomplish this is for the LEA to extend an invitation to officials of the private schools and convene a meeting with them during which LEA officials describe the ESEA programs and allowable activities available to private school students and teachers, explain the roles of public and private school officials, address the specific needs of private school students and teachers, and provide opportunities for the private school officials to ask questions and offer suggestions. A consultation process that involves an LEA simply sending a letter to private school officials explaining the purpose of federal education programs and the LEA's intent to apply for funds is not adequate consultation. Likewise, a letter describing the services that an LEA intends to provide for private school students, without any prior consultation, is not sufficient to meet the consultation requirement. For a list of suggested activities, see *J-5: Sample Consultation Checklist for Local Education Agencies.*

D-7. What topics should be discussed during the consultation process between public and private school officials?

Section 9501(c)(1) of ESEA requires that LEAs consult with appropriate private school officials on such issues as:

- how the children's needs will be identified;
- what services will be offered;
- how, where, and by whom the services will be provided;
- how the services will be assessed and how the results of the assessment will be used to improve those services;
- the size and scope of the equitable services to be provided to the eligible private school children, teachers, and other educational personnel and the amount of funds available for those services; and
- how and when the agency, consortium, or entity will make decisions about the delivery of services, including a thorough consideration and analysis of the views of the private school

officials on the provision of contract services through potential third-party providers.

See *J-6: Sample Consultation Meeting Attendance Sign-in Sheet*; see *J-7: Sample Private School Consultation Meeting Agenda*; and see *J-10: Sample Private School Consultation Planning Sheet.*

D-8. Does an offer of services from an LEA meet the requirement of consultation?

No. An offer of services by an LEA without an opportunity for timely and meaningful consultation does not meet the requirement of the law. Only after discussing key issues relating to the provision of services, identifying the needs of the students and teachers to be served, and receiving input from the private school officials, does an LEA make its final decisions with respect to the services and benefits it will provide to meet the needs of eligible private school students and teachers.

D-10. May an LEA request that private school officials provide relevant documentation in order to participate in programs?

Yes. LEAs may request documentation, as needed, from private school officials that enables the LEA to identify students who are eligible under the applicable ESEA program and the appropriate services that meet the needs of those private school students and their teachers. Such documentation might include, but not be limited to, data indicating the academic needs of students, as well as the professional development needs of teachers. However, the request for documentation should not constitute an administrative barrier that is inconsistent with the LEA's responsibility to ensure equitable participation of private school students and teachers. For an example of documentation, see *J-8: Sample Needs Assessment and Program Development Plan.*

D-16. In designing and developing programs for private school students and teachers, how should the needs of private school students and teachers be assessed?

The needs of the private school students and teachers to be served are the foundation for designing programs to serve such students and teachers, within the parameters of the particular program statute and regulations. During the consultation process, the LEA must discuss with private school officials the needs of their students and teachers as well as how best to meet those needs. For an example of a needs assessment form, see *J-8: Sample Needs Assessment and Program Development Plan.*

D-17. What is meant by "timely and meaningful" consultation?

Timely and meaningful consultation is required in order to ensure the equitable participation of private school students, teachers, and, in some programs, parents. Timely consultation begins early enough for the entire process of program design and development to be completed, for exploring the option of third-party providers, and for services to begin by the start of the school year. Timely consultation requires that LEAs provide advance notice of consultation meetings to private school officials. Meaningful consultation covers all required topics (see question D-7) and affords private school officials a genuine opportunity to express their views. Effective consultation is ongoing, two-way communication and discussion of the best ways to meet the needs of private school students and teachers under the provisions of the particular program. Consultation is significantly enhanced when public school officials provide an agenda of consultation topics, along with information about the amount of funds available for services, in advance of any consultation meeting, in order for private school officials to have the opportunity to adequately prepare for discussions.

D-18. Should consultation between the LEA and private school officials be ongoing?

Yes. In order to help ensure effective design, development, and implementation of programs, consultation between the LEA and private school officials should be ongoing throughout the school year. Issues often arise concerning service delivery and implementation, and ongoing consultation provides the means for adequately addressing them in a timely and efficient fashion.

D-20. Who is a "private school official" or "representative of private school students"?

Most often, the principal or headmaster of the private school serves as the official or representative of the students and teachers in the school. At times, the principal or headmaster may designate someone else to participate in the consultation process on behalf of the students and teachers at the school.

In the case where a group of private school officials seeks to be represented by a central office administrator, that administrator should inform in writing the LEA superintendent that she/he will serve as the designated primary contact for such schools, and that any communication and correspondence regarding ESEA programs and the participation of those private school students and teachers should be directed to her/his attention. In addition, the administrator should provide a list of the private schools that she/he represents.

D-22. What administrative tasks and paperwork are required of private school officials whose students and teachers participate in ESEA programs?

The ESEA does not impose any administrative or paperwork requirements on private school officials.

However, LEAs may request information from private school officials in order to provide services that meet the needs of their students and teachers. Therefore, there may be some paperwork that private school officials will be asked to complete to assist the LEA in administering the program on behalf of private school students and teachers. However, such paperwork should not pose an administrative burden on the private school official and should not include completing purchase orders or signing contracts.

D-24. If a private school official requests that certain services be delivered through a third party and the LEA chooses not to do so, what should the LEA include in the written explanation as to the reasons why it chose not to grant that request?

Section 9501(c)(2) of the ESEA requires an LEA to provide a "written explanation of the reasons" why it chose not to use a third party for services. An adequate explanation would address concerns expressed by private school officials about the LEA's direct services and fully explain the reasons why the LEA chose not to use a third party, such as any financial, administrative, regulatory, or statutory impediments, or the ability of the LEA to provide the services directly. The written explanation should not simply reiterate the LEA's decision but also provide reasons for the decision.

D-26. Should an LEA or SEA provide a copy of its consolidated grant application or individual program application if a private school official requests it?

Yes. The LEA or SEA should provide, in a timely manner, a copy of the consolidated application or individual program applications to those private school officials who participate in the ongoing consultation process when they request them. Such applications are a matter of public record and, therefore, generally are accessible for public review. An application can provide private school representatives with information that enhances consultation and helps them understand the scope of program activities within the LEA and the equitable participation of private school students in programs authorized under ESEA.

D-27. Are LEAs required to provide the amount of funds available for services for private school students and teachers?

Yes. LEAs must provide private school officials with the amount of funding available for services for private school students and teachers under the various ESEA programs requiring equitable participation. While LEAs generally address this topic during consultation discussions, some LEAs also provide such information through their Web sites or in written form. For an example, see *J-14: Sample Funding Allocations for Services Notification Form.*

F-2. Who pays the cost for administering programs for private school students?

Just as an LEA pays the costs for administering programs for public school students, it pays the costs for administering programs for private school students. Administrative costs are reserved from a program's total allocation (off the top) before the LEA determines the allocation for services and benefits for public and private school students and teachers.

F-9. How is the carryover of funds handled in regard to the equitable participation of private school students if an SEA permits carryover?

In general, if an LEA provided equitable services

for private school students in any given year, any carryover funds for services to private school students would be considered additional funds for that program for public and private school students in the subsequent year. Those funds then would be used, along with any other carryover funds, for both public and private school students on an equitable basis. This situation might occur, for example, if private school students and teachers did not fully participate in the ESEA program (e.g., private school teachers opted out of a proposed professional development activity), even though an equitable program was planned and offered for those students and teachers.

However, if the LEA did not provide equitable services for private school students in a given year and, as a result, there are funds remaining that should have been expended for equitable services for private school students, the LEA should use those carryover funds for private school students in the subsequent year. Those funds would be in addition to the funds that the LEA uses for private school students out of the subsequent year's allocation. This situation might occur, for example, if the LEA failed to notify or consult with private school officials about the availability of the ESEA program, or if there was a delay in the implementation of an equitable program.

F-12. May an LEA require private school officials to complete purchase orders?

No. An LEA may not require private school officials to complete purchase orders or prepare other financial requests, such as budgets, as private school officials have no authority under the equitable services provisions to obligate federal funds. Tasks related to administering services and programs funded by federal funds, such as purchasing materials for private school students and teachers, are the responsibility of the LEA. However, there may be some paperwork that private school officials will be asked to complete that is necessary in order for the LEA to administer the program. For example, private school officials may be asked to provide written recommendations on the services, programs, and materials they would like the LEA to consider purchasing and/or providing.

G-1. Who has the responsibility to implement programs for private school students, teachers, and other education personnel?

Generally, the LEA has this responsibility. However, in cases when the grant recipient is another entity, this responsibility becomes that of the SEA, educational service agency, institution of higher education, consortium of those agencies, or other entity that receives the grant. (See the note in Section B of this guidance.)

If an LEA contracts with a third-party provider to provide services and benefits to eligible private school students and teachers, the LEA remains responsible for ensuring that private school students and teachers receive equitable services and the requirements of the statute and regulations are met.

G-2. What services are offered if the needs of private school students and teachers are different from those of public school students and teachers?

The LEA offers services that meet the specific educational needs of the participating private school students and teachers and that show reasonable promise of effectiveness. The services can be different from those provided to public school students and teachers, but must be allowable services under the particular ESEA program. In addition, all services and benefits provided must be secular, neutral, and nonideological. (See section 9501(a)(1)--(2) of ESEA.)

G-3. What are some service delivery mechanisms that an LEA may use to provide equitable services?

An LEA may provide services to private school students and teachers through an employee of the LEA or through a contract with a third-party provider, an individual, an education institution, or some other agency that, in the provision of those services, is under the control and supervision of the LEA and is otherwise independent of the private school and any religious organization. (See section 9501(d)(2) of ESEA.)

G-7. May an LEA provide equitable services for private school students and teachers beyond the school year and during the summer?

Yes. In most cases, an LEA has the authority to provide services both during and beyond the school year. To the extent that private school officials have requested some services in the summer in order to better meet the needs of students and teachers, an LEA should consider accommodating such a request.

G-8. Must private school students and teachers participate in the same programs that an LEA provides for public school students and teachers?

No. Within the parameters of each ESEA program, the needs of private school students and teachers and the amount of funding available for services determine the services and programs that an LEA will offer. To the extent that the services an LEA is providing to public school students and teachers meet the needs of the private school students and teachers, an LEA could decide to provide the same services after consulting with private school officials.

The needs of the private school students and teachers to be served, not the preferences of the LEA or private school officials, determine the services to be provided.

I-1. Does Title IX, Part E, Subpart 1 contain any protections for private schools?

Yes. Title IX, Part E, Subpart 1 has provisions that contain important protections for private schools. For example, Section 9506 of ESEA states that nothing in the law shall be construed to: (a) affect any private school that does not receive funds or services under ESEA; (b) affect a home school; or (c) permit, allow, encourage, or authorize any federal control over any aspect of any private, religious, or home school.

G-12. May Title II, Part A funds be used to pay for a private school teacher's attendance at a professional conference sponsored or conducted by a faith-based organization?[13]

Yes. To the extent that the conference is part of a sustained and comprehensive secular professional development plan for the teacher, then Title II, Part A funds may be expended to pay for the portion of the costs of the conference that, as determined by the LEA, represent the secular professional development in which the teacher participated. In this case, the LEA would pay or reimburse the teacher for attendance at the conference.

NOTES

[1]Dale McDonald, PBVM, and Margaret Schultz, *The Annual Statistical Report on Schools, Enrollment and Staffing: United States Catholic Elementary and Secondary Schools 2008-2009* (Washington, DC: National Catholic Educational Association, 2009).

[2]United States Department of Education, Office of Non-Public Education, *Equitable Services for Eligible Private School Students, Teachers, and Other Educational Personnel: Non-Regulatory Guidance*, March 2009 (Washington, DC: U.S. Department of Education), §§D-6, D-7, D-8, D-16, G-2, G-7, G-8.

[3]Ibid., §§D-24, G-3.

[4]See for example, *Agostini v. Felton*, 521 U.S. 203 (1997).

[5]United States Department of Education, Office of Non-Public Education, *Equitable Services for Eligible Private School Students, Teachers, and Other Educational Personnel: Non-Regulatory Guidance*, March 2009, §D-17.

[6]Ibid., §§D-5, D-10, D-18.

[7]Ibid., §§D-4, D-20.

[8]Ibid., §D-27.

[9]Ibid., §D-26.

[10]Ibid., §§D-22, F-2, F-12, G-1.

[11]Ibid., §F-12.

[12]Ibid., §F-9.

[13]United States Department of Education, Office of Elementary and Secondary Education, *Improving Teacher Quality State Grants: Non-Regulatory Guidance*, October 2006, (Washington, DC: U.S. Department of Education), §G-12.

ACE Consulting
Stephen Perla, Director

University of Notre Dame
154 I.E.I. Building
Notre Dame, IN 46556
574-631-4646
aceconsulting@nd.edu